Book Title

Author _____   Nationality _____

Genre _____   Year _____   Pages _____

Memorable Quote	Page Number

Characters

Plot Summary

Notes

Rating

Book Title

Author

Nationality

Genre

Year

Pages

Memorable Quote	Page Number

Characters

Plot Summary

Notes

Rating

Book Title

Author _____ Nationality _____

Genre _____ Year _____ Pages _____

Memorable Quote	Page Number

Characters

Plot Summary

Notes

Rating ☆ ☆ ☆ ☆ ☆

Book Title

Author _____ Nationality _____

Genre _____ Year _____ Pages _____

Memorable Quote	Page Number

Characters

Plot Summary

Notes

Rating

Book Title

Author

Nationality

Genre

Year

Pages

Memorable Quote	Page Number

Characters

Plot Summary

Notes

Rating

Book Title

Author   Nationality

Genre   Year   Pages

Memorable Quote	Page Number

Characters

Plot Summary

Notes

Rating

Book Title

Author _____ Nationality _____

Genre _____ Year _____ Pages _____

Memorable Quote	Page Number

Characters

Plot Summary

Notes

Rating ☆ ☆ ☆ ☆ ☆

Book Title

Author _____ Nationality _____

Genre _____ Year _____ Pages _____

Memorable Quote	Page Number

Characters

Plot Summary

Notes

Rating ☆ ☆ ☆ ☆ ☆

Book Title

Author _____ Nationality _____

Genre _____ Year _____ Pages _____

Memorable Quote	Page Number

Characters

Plot Summary

Notes

Rating

Book Title

Author _____ Nationality _____

Genre _____ Year _____ Pages _____

Memorable Quote	Page Number

Characters

Plot Summary

Notes

Rating ☆ ☆ ☆ ☆ ☆

Book Title

Author

Nationality

Genre

Year

Pages

Memorable Quote	Page Number

Characters

Plot Summary

Notes

Rating

Book Title

Author _____ Nationality _____

Genre _____ Year _____ Pages _____

Memorable Quote	Page Number

Characters

Plot Summary

Notes

Rating

Book Title

Author

Nationality

Genre

Year

Pages

Memorable Quote	Page Number

Characters

Plot Summary

Notes

Rating

Book Title

Author _____ Nationality _____

Genre _____ Year _____ Pages _____

Memorable Quote	Page Number

Characters

Plot Summary

Notes

Rating

Book Title

Author

Nationality

Genre

Year

Pages

Memorable Quote	Page Number

Characters

Plot Summary

Notes

Rating ☆ ☆ ☆ ☆ ☆

Book Title

Author   Nationality

Genre   Year   Pages

Memorable Quote	Page Number

Characters

Plot Summary

Notes

Rating

Book Title

Author _____   Nationality _____

Genre _____   Year _____   Pages _____

Memorable Quote	Page Number

Characters

Plot Summary

Notes

Rating

Book Title

Author _____   Nationality _____

Genre _____   Year _____   Pages _____

Memorable Quote	Page Number

Characters

Plot Summary

Notes

Rating ☆ ☆ ☆ ☆ ☆

Book Title

Author _____   Nationality _____

Genre _____   Year _____   Pages _____

Memorable Quote	Page Number

Characters

Plot Summary

Notes

Rating

Book Title

Author

Nationality

Genre

Year

Pages

Memorable Quote	Page Number

Characters

Plot Summary

Notes

Rating

Book Title

Author _____ Nationality _____

Genre _____ Year _____ Pages _____

Memorable Quote	Page Number

Characters

Plot Summary

Notes

Rating

Book Title

Author _____   Nationality _____

Genre _____   Year _____   Pages _____

Memorable Quote	Page Number

Characters

Plot Summary

Notes

Rating

Book Title

Author

Nationality

Genre

Year

Pages

Memorable Quote	Page Number

Characters

Plot Summary

Notes

Rating

Book Title

Author _____ Nationality _____

Genre _____ Year _____ Pages _____

Memorable Quote	Page Number

Characters

Plot Summary

Notes

Rating

Book Title

Author _____   Nationality _____

Genre _____   Year _____   Pages _____

Memorable Quote	Page Number

Characters

Plot Summary

Notes

Rating

Book Title

Author _____   Nationality _____

Genre _____   Year _____   Pages _____

Memorable Quote	Page Number

Characters

Plot Summary

Notes

Rating ☆ ☆ ☆ ☆ ☆

Book Title

Author

Nationality

Genre

Year

Pages

Memorable Quote	Page Number

Characters

Plot Summary

Notes

Rating

Book Title

Author

Nationality

Genre

Year

Pages

Memorable Quote	Page Number

Characters

Plot Summary

Notes

Rating

Book Title

Author _____ Nationality _____

Genre _____ Year _____ Pages _____

Memorable Quote	Page Number

Characters

Plot Summary

Notes

Rating

Book Title

Author _____   Nationality _____

Genre _____   Year _____   Pages _____

Memorable Quote	Page Number

Characters

Plot Summary

Notes

Rating

Book Title

Author _____   Nationality _____

Genre _____   Year _____   Pages _____

Memorable Quote	Page Number

Characters

Plot Summary

Notes

Rating

Book Title

Author

Nationality

Genre

Year

Pages

Memorable Quote	Page Number

Characters

Plot Summary

Notes

Rating

Book Title

Author

Nationality

Genre

Year

Pages

Memorable Quote	Page Number

Characters

Plot Summary

Notes

Rating

Book Title

Author _____ Nationality _____

Genre _____ Year _____ Pages _____

Memorable Quote	Page Number

Characters

Plot Summary

Notes

Rating

Book Title

Author _____   Nationality _____

Genre _____   Year _____   Pages _____

Memorable Quote	Page Number

Characters

Plot Summary

Notes

Rating

Book Title

Author   Nationality

Genre   Year   Pages

Memorable Quote	Page Number

Characters

Plot Summary

Notes

Rating

Book Title

Author _____   Nationality _____

Genre _____   Year _____   Pages _____

Memorable Quote	Page Number

Characters

Plot Summary

Notes

Rating

Book Title

Author

Nationality

Genre

Year

Pages

Memorable Quote	Page Number

Characters

Plot Summary

Notes

Rating ☆ ☆ ☆ ☆ ☆

Book Title

Author

Nationality

Genre

Year

Pages

Memorable Quote	Page Number

Characters

Plot Summary

Notes

Rating

Book Title

Author   Nationality

Genre   Year   Pages

Memorable Quote	Page Number

Characters

Plot Summary

Notes

Rating 

Book Title

Author _____   Nationality _____

Genre _____   Year _____   Pages _____

Memorable Quote	Page Number

Characters

Plot Summary

Notes

Rating

Book Title

Author   Nationality

Genre   Year   Pages

Memorable Quote	Page Number

Characters

Plot Summary

Notes

Rating

Book Title

Author _____   Nationality _____

Genre _____   Year _____   Pages _____

Memorable Quote	Page Number

Characters

Plot Summary

Notes

Rating ☆ ☆ ☆ ☆ ☆

Book Title

Author   Nationality

Genre   Year   Pages

Memorable Quote	Page Number

Characters

Plot Summary

Notes

Rating   ☆ ☆ ☆ ☆ ☆

Book Title

Author

Nationality

Genre

Year

Pages

Memorable Quote	Page Number

Characters

Plot Summary

Notes

Rating

Book Title

Author _____   Nationality _____

Genre _____   Year _____   Pages _____

Memorable Quote	Page Number

Characters

Plot Summary

Notes

Rating

Book Title

Author _____   Nationality _____

Genre _____   Year _____   Pages _____

Memorable Quote	Page Number

Characters

Plot Summary

Notes

Rating

Book Title

Author   Nationality

Genre   Year   Pages

Memorable Quote	Page Number

Characters

Plot Summary

Notes

Rating

Book Title

Author   Nationality

Genre   Year   Pages

Memorable Quote	Page Number

Characters

Plot Summary

Notes

Rating   ☆ ☆ ☆ ☆ ☆

Book Title

Author _____   Nationality _____

Genre _____   Year _____   Pages _____

Memorable Quote	Page Number

Characters

Plot Summary

Notes

Rating

Book Title

Author _____   Nationality _____

Genre _____   Year _____   Pages _____

Memorable Quote	Page Number

Characters

Plot Summary

Notes

Rating

Book Title

Author   Nationality

Genre   Year   Pages

Memorable Quote	Page Number

Characters

Plot Summary

Notes

Rating

Book Title

Author _____   Nationality _____

Genre _____   Year _____   Pages _____

Memorable Quote	Page Number

Characters

Plot Summary

Notes

Rating

Book Title

Author

Nationality

Genre

Year

Pages

Memorable Quote	Page Number

Characters

Plot Summary

Notes

Rating

Book Title

Author _____ Nationality _____

Genre _____ Year _____ Pages _____

Memorable Quote	Page Number

Characters

Plot Summary

Notes

Rating ☆ ☆ ☆ ☆ ☆

Book Title

Author _____   Nationality _____

Genre _____   Year _____   Pages _____

Memorable Quote	Page Number

Characters

Plot Summary

Notes

Rating

Book Title

Author _____   Nationality _____

Genre _____   Year _____   Pages _____

Memorable Quote	Page Number

Characters

Plot Summary

Notes

Rating ☆ ☆ ☆ ☆ ☆

Book Title

Author _____ Nationality _____

Genre _____ Year _____ Pages _____

Memorable Quote	Page Number

Characters

Plot Summary

Notes

Rating

Book Title

Author _____   Nationality _____

Genre _____   Year _____   Pages _____

Memorable Quote	Page Number

Characters

Plot Summary

Notes

Rating

Book Title

Author

Nationality

Genre

Year

Pages

Memorable Quote	Page Number

Characters

Plot Summary

Notes

Rating

Book Title

Author _____ Nationality _____

Genre _____ Year _____ Pages _____

Memorable Quote	Page Number

Characters

Plot Summary

Notes

Rating ☆ ☆ ☆ ☆ ☆

Book Title

Author _____   Nationality _____

Genre _____   Year _____   Pages _____

Memorable Quote	Page Number

Characters

Plot Summary

Notes

Rating ☆ ☆ ☆ ☆ ☆

Book Title

Author

Nationality

Genre

Year

Pages

Memorable Quote	Page Number

Characters

Plot Summary

Notes

Rating

Book Title

Author

Nationality

Genre

Year

Pages

Memorable Quote	Page Number

Characters

Plot Summary

Notes

Rating ☆ ☆ ☆ ☆ ☆

Book Title

Author

Nationality

Genre

Year

Pages

Memorable Quote	Page Number

Characters

Plot Summary

Notes

Rating

Book Title

Author

Nationality

Genre

Year

Pages

Memorable Quote	Page Number

Characters

Plot Summary

Notes

Rating

Book Title

Author _____ Nationality _____

Genre _____ Year _____ Pages _____

Memorable Quote	Page Number

Characters

Plot Summary

Notes

Rating

Book Title

Author

Nationality

Genre

Year

Pages

Memorable Quote	Page Number

Characters

Plot Summary

Notes

Rating

Book Title

Author

Nationality

Genre

Year

Pages

Memorable Quote	Page Number

Characters

Plot Summary

Notes

Rating

Book Title

Author _____   Nationality _____

Genre _____   Year _____   Pages _____

Memorable Quote	Page Number

Characters

Plot Summary

Notes

Rating ☆ ☆ ☆ ☆ ☆

Book Title

Author _____ Nationality _____

Genre _____ Year _____ Pages _____

Memorable Quote	Page Number

Characters

Plot Summary

Notes

Rating

Book Title

Author

Nationality

Genre

Year

Pages

Memorable Quote	Page Number

Characters

Plot Summary

Notes

Rating

Book Title

Author _____   Nationality _____

Genre _____   Year _____   Pages _____

Memorable Quote	Page Number

Characters

Plot Summary

Notes

Rating ☆ ☆ ☆ ☆ ☆

Book Title

Author

Nationality

Genre

Year

Pages

Memorable Quote	Page Number

Characters

Plot Summary

Notes

Rating

Book Title

Author _____ Nationality _____

Genre _____ Year _____ Pages _____

Memorable Quote	Page Number

Characters

Plot Summary

Notes

Rating

Book Title

Author   Nationality

Genre   Year   Pages

Memorable Quote	Page Number

Characters

Plot Summary

Notes

Rating ☆ ☆ ☆ ☆ ☆

Book Title

Author _____   Nationality _____

Genre _____   Year _____   Pages _____

Memorable Quote	Page Number

Characters

Plot Summary

Notes

Rating ☆ ☆ ☆ ☆ ☆

Book Title

Author _____   Nationality _____

Genre _____   Year _____   Pages _____

Memorable Quote	Page Number

Characters

Plot Summary

Notes

Rating

Book Title

Author

Nationality

Genre

Year

Pages

Memorable Quote	Page Number

Characters

Plot Summary

Notes

Rating ☆ ☆ ☆ ☆ ☆

Book Title

Author _____   Nationality _____

Genre _____   Year _____   Pages _____

Memorable Quote	Page Number

Characters

Plot Summary

Notes

Rating

Book Title

Author _____   Nationality _____

Genre _____   Year _____   Pages _____

Memorable Quote	Page Number

Characters

Plot Summary

Notes

Rating

Book Title

Author

Nationality

Genre

Year

Pages

Memorable Quote	Page Number

Characters

Plot Summary

Notes

Rating

Book Title

Author

Nationality

Genre

Year

Pages

Memorable Quote	Page Number

Characters

Plot Summary

Notes

Rating

Book Title

Author _____ Nationality _____

Genre _____ Year _____ Pages _____

Memorable Quote	Page Number

Characters

Plot Summary

Notes

Rating ☆ ☆ ☆ ☆ ☆

Book Title

Author _____   Nationality _____

Genre _____   Year _____   Pages _____

Memorable Quote	Page Number

Characters

Plot Summary

Notes

Rating ☆ ☆ ☆ ☆ ☆

Book Title

Author _____   Nationality _____

Genre _____   Year _____   Pages _____

Memorable Quote	Page Number

Characters

Plot Summary

Notes

Rating ☆ ☆ ☆ ☆ ☆

Book Title

Author _____ Nationality _____

Genre _____ Year _____ Pages _____

Memorable Quote	Page Number

Characters

Plot Summary

Notes

Rating

Book Title

Author _____ Nationality _____

Genre _____ Year _____ Pages _____

Memorable Quote	Page Number

Characters

Plot Summary

Notes

Rating ☆ ☆ ☆ ☆ ☆

Book Title

Author _____ Nationality _____

Genre _____ Year _____ Pages _____

Memorable Quote	Page Number

Characters

Plot Summary

Notes

Rating

Book Title

Author _____   Nationality _____

Genre _____   Year _____   Pages _____

Memorable Quote	Page Number

Characters

Plot Summary

Notes

Rating

Book Title

Author _____ Nationality _____

Genre _____ Year _____ Pages _____

Memorable Quote	Page Number

Characters

Plot Summary

Notes

Rating

Book Title

Author _____   Nationality _____

Genre _____   Year _____   Pages _____

Memorable Quote	Page Number

Characters

Plot Summary

Notes

Rating

Book Title

Author

Nationality

Genre

Year

Pages

Memorable Quote	Page Number

Characters

Plot Summary

Notes

Rating

Book Title

Author _____ Nationality _____

Genre _____ Year _____ Pages _____

Memorable Quote	Page Number

Characters

Plot Summary

Notes

Rating

Book Title

Author _____ Nationality _____

Genre _____ Year _____ Pages _____

Memorable Quote	Page Number

Characters

Plot Summary

Notes

Rating ☆ ☆ ☆ ☆ ☆

Book Title

Author

Nationality

Genre

Year

Pages

Memorable Quote	Page Number

Characters

Plot Summary

Notes

Rating

Book Title

Author _____   Nationality _____

Genre _____   Year _____   Pages _____

Memorable Quote	Page Number

Characters

Plot Summary

Notes

Rating

Book Title

Author _____   Nationality _____

Genre _____   Year _____   Pages _____

Memorable Quote	Page Number

Characters

Plot Summary

Notes

Rating

Book Title

Author

Nationality

Genre

Year

Pages

Memorable Quote	Page Number

Characters

Plot Summary

Notes

Rating

Book Title

Author _____ Nationality _____

Genre _____ Year _____ Pages _____

Memorable Quote	Page Number

Characters

Plot Summary

Notes

Rating